A Book of Days

Valerie Greeley

A BOOK OF DAYS

*A perpetual diary
and birthday book
to remind you
of special days*

Blackie

For Tony and Patrick

Thirty day hath September
April, June and November.
February hath twenty eight alone
And all the rest have thirty one

CHRONICLES OF ENGLAND 1570

JANUARY

| 1 |

| 2 |

| 3 |

| 4 |

Magpie in the Snow

White land
Black veins of branches
Dead blue eye of the sky
Magpie flicks tail
Dances
Winks a living eye.

MICHAEL TANNER

5

6

7

8

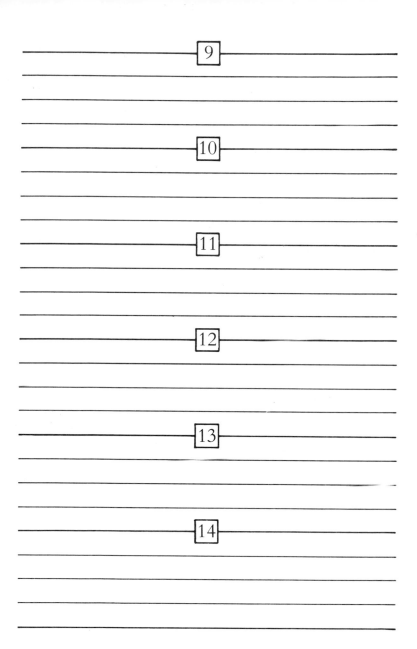

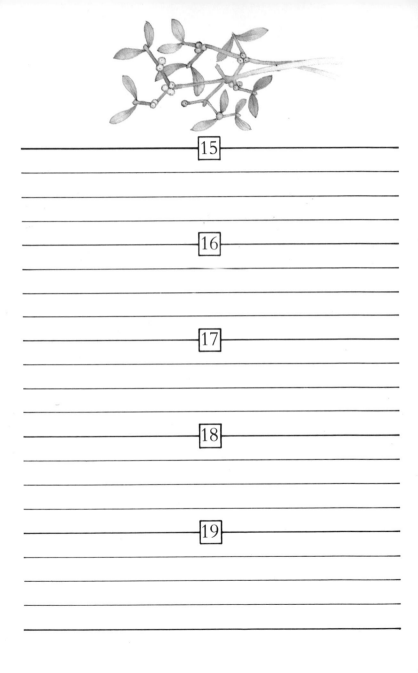

15

16

17

18

19

The Snowflake
Before I melt,
Come, look at me!
This lovely icy filigree!
Of a great forest
In one night
I make a wilderness of white:
By skyey cold
Of crystals made,
All softly, on
Your finger laid,
I pause, that you
My beauty see:
Breathe, and I vanish
Instantly.

WALTER DE LA MARE

23

24

25

26

27

28

29

30

31

FEBRUARY

1

2

3

4

| 5 |
| 6 |
| 7 |
| 8 |
| 9 |
| 10 |

One I love, two I love,
Three I love I say;
Four I love with all my heart,
Five I cast away.
Six he loves, seven she loves,
Eight they love together,
Nine he comes, ten he tarries,
Eleven he woos, and twelve he marries.

ANON

11

12

13

14

15

16

17

18

19

21

22

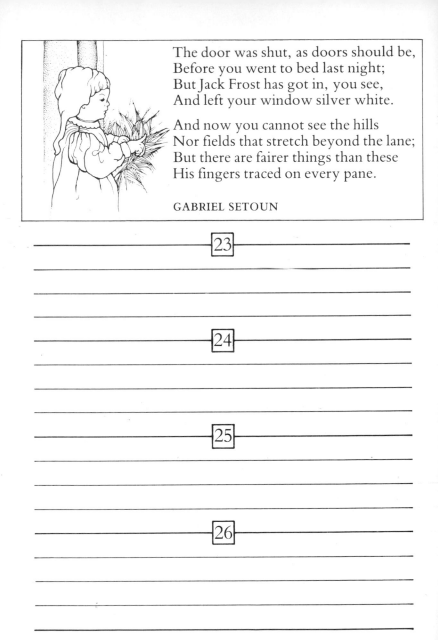

The door was shut, as doors should be,
Before you went to bed last night;
But Jack Frost has got in, you see,
And left your window silver white.

And now you cannot see the hills
Nor fields that stretch beyond the lane;
But there are fairer things than these
His fingers traced on every pane.

GABRIEL SETOUN

23

24

25

26

MARCH

1

2

3

4

Now the sleeping creatures waken – waken, waken;
Blossoms with soft winds are shaken – shaken, shaken;
Squirrels scamper and the hare
Runs races which the children share
Till their shouting fills the air.

RAYMOND WILSON

5

6

7

March brings breezes loud and shrill,
Stirs the dancing daffodil.

SARA COLERIDGE

14

15

16

17

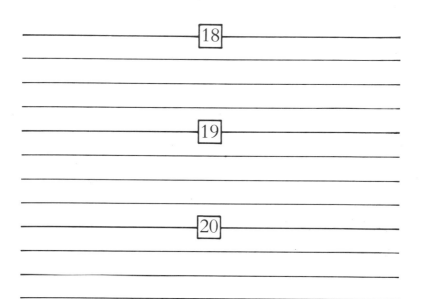

21

22

23

24

25

26

27

28

29

30

31

EASTER

For, lo, the winter is past,
The rain is over and gone;
The flowers appear on the earth;
The time of the singing
Of birds is come
And the voice of the turtle
Is heard in our land.

THE SONG OF SOLOMON

The joy that people feel in spring when light, warmth and colour return to the world has always been a good reason to celebrate. The birth of the first lambs, the hatching of baby birds and buds bursting into tender green leaves all show that the bleak winter months are over at last.

Even the earliest civilisations marked the yearly renewal of life with spring festivals and when the first Christians began to celebrate the most important festival in their religious year – the time of Christ's resurrection – the traditions of pagan festivals would have been a well-established part of their everyday life. It was a natural thing for them to adopt some of the existing customs for their own celebrations.

Among these was the giving of eggs, universal symbols of new life and fertility. A simple gift of eggs would have been a welcome treat for orthodox Christians who had denied themselves eggs and butter during their Lenten fast. But nowadays, when Lent is not so strictly observed, we usually give each other chocolate eggs at Easter.

For most people the only reminders of traditional fasting are Pancake Day, when all the remaining eggs and butter in the house would have been used up, and Mardi Gras (literally Fat Tuesday) the last big party before Easter, when carnivals are held in many countries.

In Eastern Europe, Easter eggs are decorated in bright traditional patterns, often in glowing reds. Great care and skill goes into painting or waxing and dyeing them. The most extravagant and spectacular decorated Easter eggs must be the ones made of gold and precious stones for the Russian royal family by the jeweller Fabergé.

In some European countries the Easter Hare is said to bring eggs and hide them around the house and garden for the children to find on Easter morning. (In America the Easter Bunny seems to have taken over from the Hare.) The hare itself is a fertility symbol, dedicated to the north European goddess Eostre, from whose name the word Easter derives.

Other names for Easter, such as the French pâques and Italian pasqua come from the Greek word for Passover. This is because Jesus came to Jerusalem to celebrate Passover immediately before his betrayal and crucifixion. The association with Passover still exists in the English language in our word "paschal".

Unlike Passover, Easter does not have a fixed date. It once used to be celebrated on the first Sunday after Passover, but in 325 leaders of the Christian church at the Council of Nicaea decided that Easter should fall on the Sunday following the first full moon after the spring equinox (March 21st). As a result, Easter Sunday may be as early as 22nd March or as late as 25th April.

Another symbol of Easter and the coming of spring is fire. A "paschal" candle is lit on Easter Eve to represent the light which Christ brought to the world. More obviously pagan in origin is the tradition of Easter bonfires. These are lit on hilltops or in churchyards on Easter Saturday. People may leap over the fire for good luck, or carry burning logs through the fields, believing that where the firelight casts its glow the ground will be especially fertile for the coming year.

APRIL

1

2

3

4

5

6

7

Little Lamb, who made thee,
Dost thou know who made thee,
Gave thee life and bade thee feed
By the stream and o'er the mead;
Gave thee clothing of delight,
Softest clothing, woolly, bright;

WILLIAM BLAKE

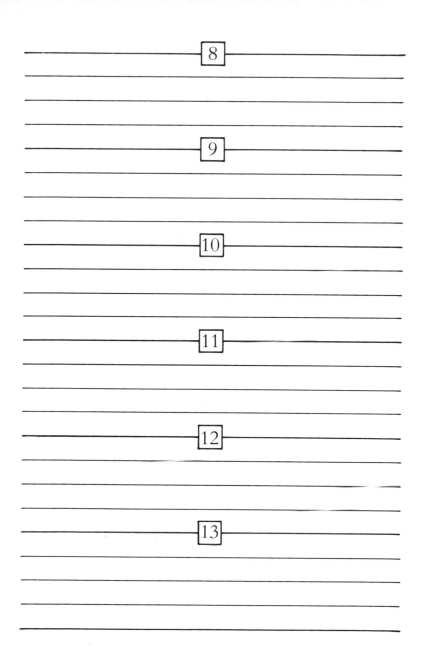

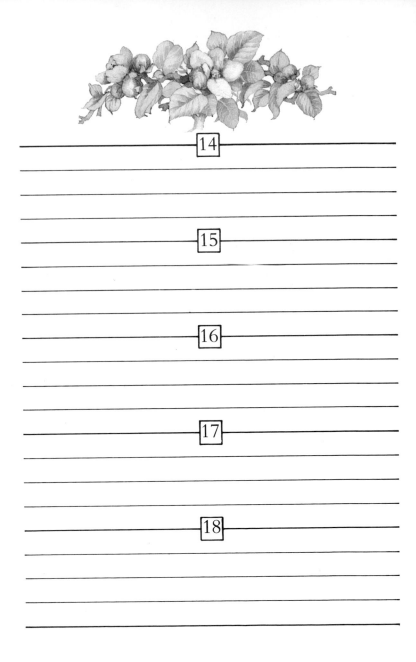

14

15

16

17

18

It was a lover and his lass,
With a hey, and a ho, and a hey nonino,
That o'er the green corn-field did pass,
In the spring time, the only pretty ring time,
When birds do sing, hey ding a ding, ding;
Sweet lovers love the spring.

SHAKESPEARE

_____ 22 _____
_____
_____
_____

_____ 23 _____
_____
_____
_____

_____ 24 _____
_____
_____
_____

25

26

27

28

29

30

MAY

1

2

3

4

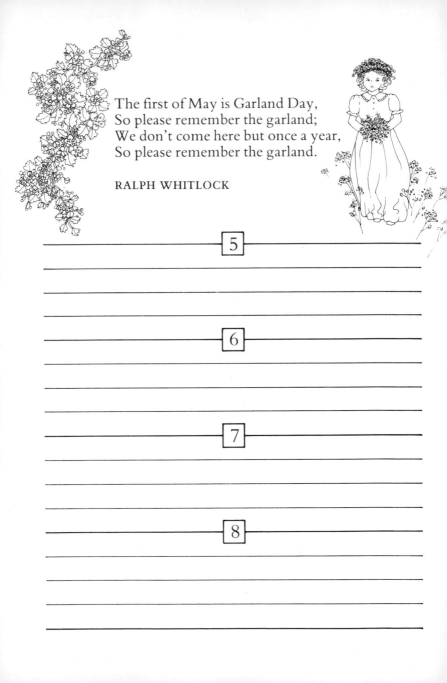

The first of May is Garland Day,
So please remember the garland;
We don't come here but once a year,
So please remember the garland.

RALPH WHITLOCK

5

6

7

8

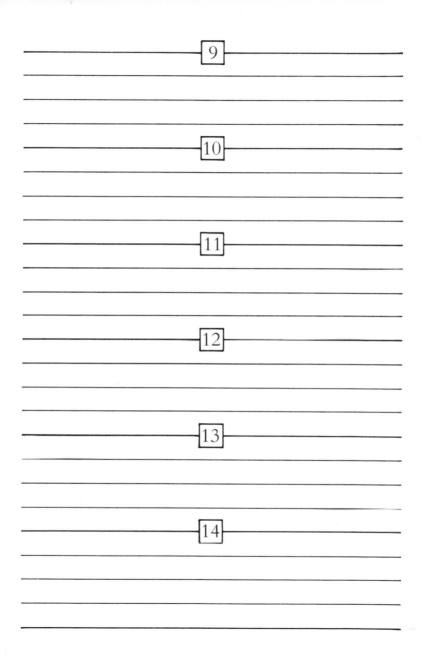

The rabbit has a charming face;
Its private life is a disgrace.
I really dare not name to you
The awful things that rabbits do –

15

ANON

16

17

18

19

21

22

23

24

25

26

27

28

29

30

31

Hurt no living thing;
Ladybird, nor butterfly,
Nor moth with dusty wing.
Nor cricket chirping cheerily,
Nor grasshopper so light of leap,
Nor dancing gnat, nor beetle fat,
Nor harmless worms that creep.

CHRISTINA ROSSETTI

JUNE

1

2

3

4

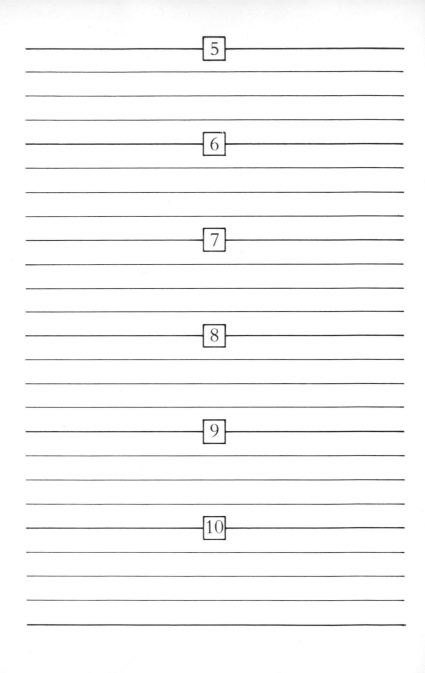

Dandelion, dandelion,
Dandelion flower,
If I breathe upon thee
Pray tell me the hour.

Little child, little child,
Little child I pray
Breathe but gently on me
Lest you blow the time away.

GARETH OWEN

Be kind and tender to the Frog,
And do not call him names,
As "slimy-skin", or "Pollywog"
Or likewise "Uncle James",
Or "Gape-a-grin", or "Toad-gone-wrong",
Or "Billy Bandy-knees";
The frog is justly sensitive
To epithets like these.

HILAIRE BELLOC

13

14

15

16

17

Well by reason men call it maie,
The Daisie, or else the Eye of the Daie.

GEOFFREY CHAUCER

21

22

23

24

25

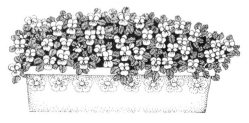

JULY

1

2

3

4

I know a bank where the wild thyme blows,
Where oxlips and the nodding violet grows,
Quite overcanopied with luscious woodbine,
With sweet musk-roses and with eglantine.

WILLIAM SHAKESPEARE

5

6

7

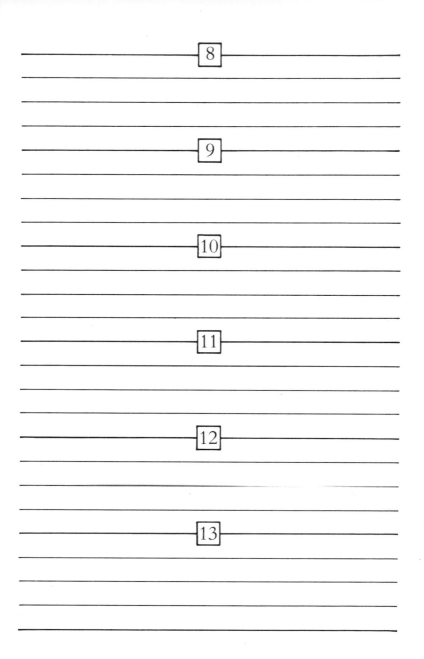

14

15

16

The Kingfisher
It was the Rainbow gave thee birth,
And left thee all her lovely hues;
And, as her mother's name was Tears,
So runs it in my blood to choose
For haunts the lonely pools, and keep
In company with trees that weep.

W H DAVIES

17

18

19

20

21

22

23

24

25

26

27

28

29

30

31

AUGUST

1

2

3

4

5

6

7

8

9

10

11

12

13

In mac, sou'wester and gum boots, he
stands under spouts, shakes a wet tree,
leaps into puddles it never can be
too wet for the ducks or William Roy.

RAYMOND O'MALLEY

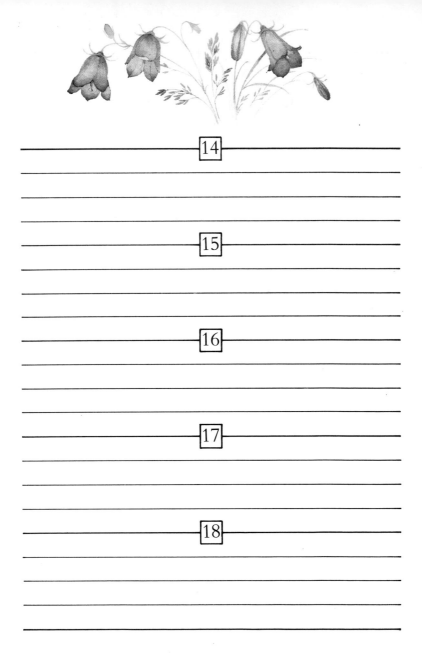

14

15

16

17

18

22

23

24

25

26

27

28

29

30

31

The Swallow
Fly away, fly away, over the sea,
Sun-loving swallow, for summer is done.
Come again, come again, come back to me,
Bringing the summer and bringing the sun.

CHRISTINA ROSSETTI

SEPTEMBER

1

2

3

4

To a Squirrel at Kyle-Na-No
Come play with me;
Why should you run
Through the shaking tree
As though I'd a gun
To strike you dead?
When all I would do
Is to scratch your head
And let you go.

W B YEATS

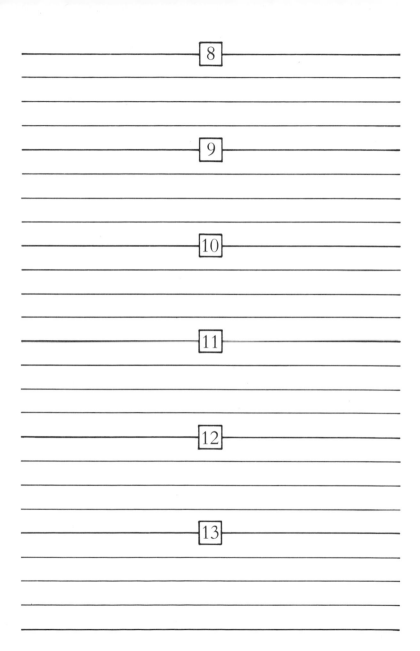

Season of mists and
mellow fruitfulness

JOHN KEATS

14

15

16

17

18

19

20

21

22

23

24

25

26

27

OCTOBER

1

2

3

4

Little wind, blow on the hill-top,
Little wind, blow down the plain;
Little wind, blow up the sunshine,
Little wind, blow off the rain.

KATE GREENAWAY

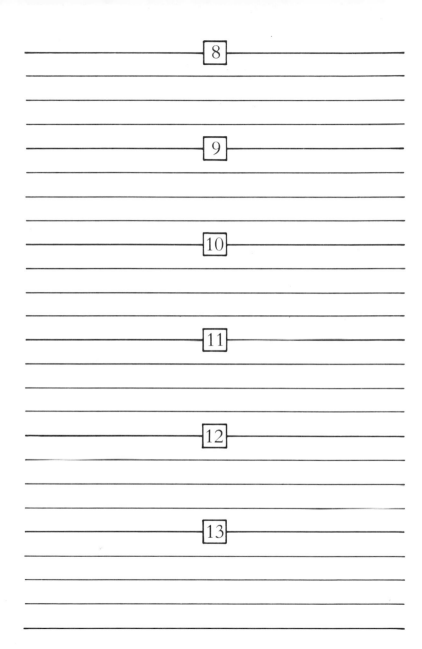

14

15

16

17

18

_22_

_23_

_24_

_25_

Beech Leaves

In autumn down the beechwood path
The leaves lie thick upon the ground.
It's there I love to kick my way
And hear their crisp and crashing sound.

JAMES REEVES

26

27

28

29

30

31

NOVEMBER

1

2

3

4

The Starlings

I

Early in spring time, on raw and windy mornings,
Beneath the freezing house-eaves I heard the starlings sing –
"Ah dreary March month, is this then a time for building wearily?
Sad, sad, to think that the year is but begun!"

II

Late in the autumn, on still and cloudless evenings,
Among the golden reed-beds I heard the starlings sing –
"Ah that sweet March month, when we and our mates were courting merrily;
Sad, sad, to think the year is all but done!"

CHARLES KINGSLEY

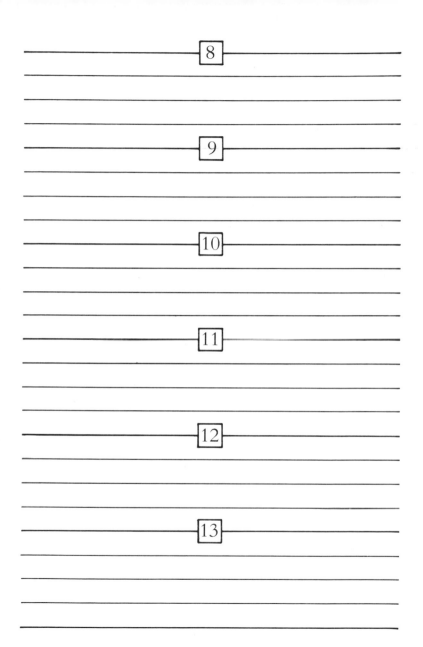

Bite, frost, bite!
You roll away from the light
The blue wood-louse and the plump dormouse,
And the bees are stilled and the flies are killed,
And you bite far into the heart of the house,
But not into mine.

LORD TENNYSON

14

15

16

17

18

22

23

24

Ice in November to bear a duck
The rest of the winter'll be slush and muck.

OLD SAYING

25

26

27

28

29

30

DECEMBER

1

2

3

4

5

6

7

8

Winter is the king of showmen,
Turning tree stumps into snow men
And houses into birthday cakes
And spreading sugar over lakes.
Smooth and clean and frosty white,
The world looks good enough to bite.
That's the season to be young,
Catching snowflakes on your tongue.

OGDEN NASH

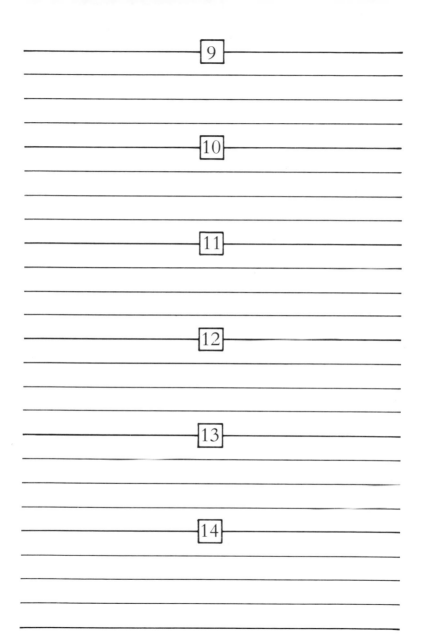

15

16

17

18

19

20

21

And feathered in fire
Where ghosts the moon,
A robin shrills
His lonely tune.

WALTER DE LA MARE

22

23

24

25

26

27

28

29

30

31

The holly and the ivy,
When they are both full grown,
Of all the trees that are in the wood,
The holly bears the crown.

TRADITIONAL CAROL

CHRISTMAS

In the bleak mid-winter
Frosty wind made moan

CHRISTINA ROSSETTI

Before Christianity, mid-winter was traditionally a time of merry-making and feasting for the people of Europe. In the fourth century, when Pope Julius I decided to establish 25th December as the feast of the birth of Christ, he was really adapting two important pagan festivals: the Roman feast of Saturnalia and the Norse feast of Yule. Both of these took place in late December and involved lights, fires and the bringing of greenery into the house.

Many of the traditions and customs which we now regard as essential to Christmas have ancient pagan origins. Mistletoe, for example, was regarded as a magical plant and, like holly, was thought to offer protection from thunder and lightning. Holly was also a symbol of eternal life.

Most homes feature a decorated tree at Christmas time. This is a German custom thought to have its origins in the eighth century, although Martin Luther was probably the first person to decorate a Christmas tree with candles to remind children of the stars in the heavens. Christmas trees only really became popular in Britain after 1841, the year in which Prince Albert, Queen Victoria's German husband, made a decorated tree the centre of the royal family's Christmas celebrations.

Gift giving was a feature of the Roman festival of Saturnalia and is, of course, associated with the Wise Men who brought gifts of gold, frankincense and myrrh to the

infant Jesus. However, for most children today the arrival
of gaily wrapped gifts on 25th December is linked with the
jolly, red-robed figure of Father Christmas.

Father Christmas, or Santa Claus, as he is also
known, is a character based primarily on the legends
surrounding Saint Nicholas who was the bishop of Myra
in Asia Minor during the fourth century. Nicholas, who
was very wealthy, wanted to serve God and to help others
who were less fortunate than himself. One of the most
famous stories of his generosity tells how he helped a
merchant who could not afford dowries for his three
daughters. One morning the eldest of the girls discovered
a bag of gold in one of the stockings which she had hung
by the chimney to dry and so she was able to marry.

The second daughter received a similar gift of gold
and she too married. Her father wanted to know who was
helping him in this unusual way and one night while he
was keeping watch he saw the bishop throwing a bag of
gold down the chimney for his third daughter. The story
spread and thus we have the traditions of Christmas
stockings and Father Christmas's strange means of entry
into houses.

The use of Christmas cards to convey the season's greetings is, relatively speaking, quite a new custom. The Penny Post, which was introduced in 1840, made it inexpensive and easy for people to send messages to each other. However, Sir Henry Cole, the director of the Victoria and Albert Museum, had little time for writing letters and so he asked an artist, John Horsley, to design a card for Christmas which could carry a printed message. Although only a thousand copies of the first card were printed, the idea caught on and spread rapidly and now the traditional scenes of snow and robins which featured on early English cards are used throughout the world, even in countries where there are no robins and hardly any snow.

BIRTHSTONES

JANUARY *Garnet*
Red, sometimes with a violet, orange or brown tint
Its name is derived from the Latin word for grain,
because of the grain-like shape in which crystals are
sometimes found.

FEBRUARY *Amethyst* Violet or purple
Amethyst is found in volcanic rock, usually lining a
small cavity. Its name comes from a Greek word
meaning "not drunken", and it was supposed to
protect the wearer against intoxication. Many
supernatural qualities are attributed to this stone.

MARCH *Aquamarine* Light greenish blue
Its name is derived from Latin and means water of
the sea. Aquamarine is a favourite good luck charm
for sailors. The darker the blue colour, the more
valuable the stone.

APRIL *Diamond* Usually colourless
The name comes from the Greek word "adamas",
meaning unconquerable. It is the hardest of all the
minerals. Many cut diamonds are famous for their
size and beauty, such as the Koh-i-Noor
("Mountain of Light") which is now part of the
British Crown Jewels.

MAY *Emerald* Light or dark green
Its name is taken from the Greek word for green
stone, "smaragdos". The darker the green colour
of the stone, the more precious it is.

JUNE *Pearl* Usually silvery pink or cream
Pearls are formed by molluscs as a protective
barrier around a foreign body, such as a tiny
parasite or grain of sand which has invaded the
mollusc's shell. The iridescence of pearls is thought
to be due to the many, thin, uneven layers of which
they are formed.

JULY *Ruby* Red
The most precious rubies are said to be the colour
of pigeons' blood – red with a blue tint. The Latin
word "rubeus" means red. Rubies are very hard,
and although less hard than diamonds, large rubies
are rarer and so are the most expensive of gems.

AUGUST *Peridot* Greenish or yellowish brown
Also called chrysolite, from the Greek name for a
gold stone. These gems were brought to Europe in
the Middle Ages by the Crusaders and have often
been used to decorate religious artifacts.

SEPTEMBER *Sapphire* Usually blue
The most sought-after colour is pure cornflower
blue. The name comes from a Greek word
"sappheiros", probably meaning the blue stone
lapis lazuli. The largest cut sapphire in the world is
the Star of India.

OCTOBER *Opal*
White or grey with blue, green and orange
iridescence
The name comes from a Sanskrit word meaning
precious stone. Many superstitions surround this
stone. In the East it represents loyalty and hope,
but in the West it is thought to be unlucky.

NOVEMBER *Topaz* Normally reddish yellow
Its name is taken from an island in the Red Sea
called Topagos. Some very large stones have been
found, weighing several pounds. The Braganza is a
famous 1640 carat topaz in the Portuguese crown.

DECEMBER *Turquoise*
It acquired its name, meaning "Turkish stone"
because the trade routes on which it was brought to
Europe passed through Turkey, although the best
examples are found in Iran. It was traditionally
used to decorate amulets and was popular in the
Victorian era as an embellishment on chinoiserie.

THE ZODIAC

The Zodiac derives its name from a Greek word meaning "living creatures", and this was the name given by Aristotle to the images pictured in the stars. In 800 BC the Babylonians, who were fascinated by astrology, thought that the earth stood still and the planets moved around it. They believed that the sun in its path across the sky visited twelve different groups of stars, each for about 30 days.

The twelve groups named after the images in the stars are known as the signs of the zodiac. Each has its own distinctive character, temperament and natural way of acting. The Sun, Moon and eight planets rule the star signs and give the basic character.

The four elements which give the temperament are:
FIRE *(gives warmth, light, burns, consumes)*
People with fire as their element tend to be energetic and creative, though sometimes impetuous and impatient. Quick thinking, they can also be outspoken. They are emotionally warm to others. (Aries, Leo, Sagittarius).

EARTH *(supportive, heavy, a provider)*
"Earth" people are slow and ponderous, but once a decision has been made, they stick with it. They are practical, intelligent and good at organizing. (Taurus, Virgo, Capricorn)

WATER *(a sustaining source of refreshment that reflects the world and needs a container)*
Emotional, intuitive, often needing direction or a purpose to their lives, these people are impressionable, imaginative and sensitive. (Cancer, Scorpio, Pisces).

AIR
Good in social situations. Strong mental abilities. People who have air as their main element are good advisers and usually intellectual. (Gemini, Libra, Aquarius).

Three qualities of movement show how a person's natural way of acting can be predicted in each sign:

CARDINAL *(pure movement)* – Aries, Cancer, Libra, Capricorn.
Direct and decisive action, purposeful and likes initiating. May be restless and domineering, but likes action and is good at organizing new enterprises.

FIXED *(static)* – Taurus, Leo, Scorpio, Aquarius.
Persistent and determined. Success through perseverance. Constant and reliable, though can be stubborn and rigid. Capable of sustained effort, often planning into the future.

MUTABLE *(a mixture of both, adaptable)* – Gemini, Virgo, Sagittarius, Pisces.
Can deal with a great variety of experiences and ideas, and is able to blend into the surroundings. Flexible and good in emergencies. Can be trapped in past memories, but is always resourceful.

The ruling planets and their influences:

⊙ THE SUN	☾ THE MOON
Power and vitality.	Responsiveness and instinct
☿ MERCURY	♀ VENUS
Intellect and perceptiveness	Emotion and power to love
♂ MARS	♃ JUPITER
Energy and initiative	Optimism and generosity
♄ SATURN	♅ URANUS
Ambition mixed with caution	Strong will and versatility
♆ NEPTUNE	♇ PLUTO
Sensitivity and idealism	Secretiveness and power

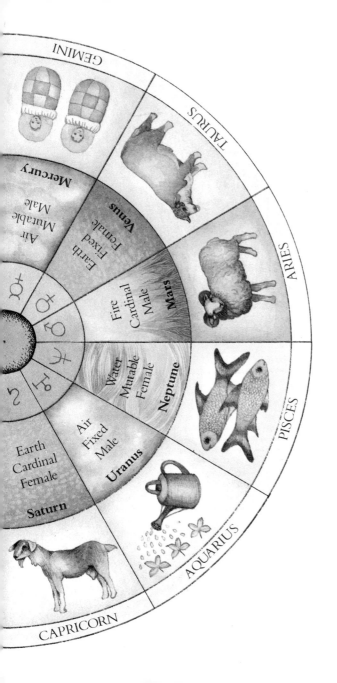

GEMINI

TAURUS

ARIES

PISCES

AQUARIUS

CAPRICORN

Mercury

Air
Mutable
Male

Venus
Earth
Fixed
Female

Mars
Fire
Cardinal
Male

Neptune
Water
Mutable
Female

Uranus
Air
Fixed
Male

Saturn
Earth
Cardinal
Female

ARIES *March 21st-April 20th*
Forceful · Energetic · Eager · Sometimes too hasty ·
Competitive · Likes to lead · Impatient · Quick to anger ·
Direct · Honest · Warm · Generous · Optimistic.

TAURUS *April 21st-May 21st*
Stubborn · Determined · Loyal · Normally slow to anger,
with occasional towering rages · Practical · Taciturn ·
Home-loving · Loves to cook and eat good food · Patient ·
Stoic.

GEMINI *May 22nd-June 21st*
Likes variety · Adaptable · Articulate · Analytical · Good
sense of humour · Can be fickle · Alert · Quick-thinking ·
Gossipy · Frank · Likes a large circle of friends.

CANCER *June 22nd-July 23rd*
Moody · Maternal · Tenacious · Thrifty · Likes to hoard
things · Secretive · Emotional · Craves security · Sensitive ·
Nostalgic · Conservative · A worrier · A home-maker · Has a
"loony" sense of humour.

LEO *July 24th-August 23rd*
Bold · Proud · Can be vain · Likes to be in charge · Brave ·
Craves love and admiration · Susceptible to flattery · Open ·
Generous · Passionate · Romantic · Extravagant · A good
host.

VIRGO *August 24th-September 23rd*
Dutiful · Hard-working · Sometimes too serious · Reserved ·
A worrier · Resourceful · Fastidious · Practical · Self-critical ·
Neat · Takes care of appearance.

LIBRA *September 24th-October 23rd*
A charmer · Romantic · Sociable · Fun-loving · Balanced ·
Can be indecisive · Good-natured · Gullible · Sometimes
self-indulgent · Has swings of mood · Argumentative ·
Honest.

SCORPIO *October 24th-November 22nd*
Secretive · Perceptive · Strong feelings of like and dislike ·
Reserved · Inscrutable · Can be ruthless · Devoted to family
and friends · Passionate.

SAGITTARIUS *November 23rd-December 21st*
Energetic · Has large appetites · Restless · Candid · Rational ·
Lacks constraint · Ebullient · Sometimes tactless, but
well-meaning · Can be clumsy · Generous · Sincere ·
Idealistic.

CAPRICORN *December 22nd-January 20th*
Patient · Dogged · Serious · Sometimes aloof · Practical ·
Competitive · Aims for long-term goals · Ambitious ·
Self-disciplined · Quiet · Tough · Dependable.

AQUARIUS *January 21st-February 19th*
A teacher · Likes to take a world view of events · Inventive ·
Sociable · Intuitive, sometimes psychic · Talkative · Idealistic
· Non-conformist · Unpredictable · Analytic · Inquisitive.

PISCES *February 20th-March 20th*
Compassionate · A philosopher · Spiritual · Has hidden
depths · Acts on instinct · Adaptable to change · Creative ·
Likes solitude · Sensual · Sensitive · Gentle · Moody · Musical
· Artistic · Imaginative · Elusive.

PERSONAL NOTES

Name

_____

Address

_____

_____

_____

_____

_____

Private telephone number

_____

Business telephone number

_____

Important telephone numbers

_____   _____

_____   _____

_____   _____

Driving licence number

_____

National Insurance number

_____

Blood group

_____

Allergies

_____

Passport number

_____

Credit card numbers

_____

_____

Bank account number

_____

Building society account number

_____

THANKS
My thanks to: Rosemary Lanning for help with the text,
encouragement and editorial assistance, to my husband, Tony
Corrigan, for his help with poetry selection and the Christmas text, and
last but not least for his unstinting practical support and
encouragement.

ACKNOWLEDGEMENTS

The publishers gratefully acknowledge permission to reprint copyright material from the following:

Magpie in the Snow by Michael Tanner from *The Beaver Book of Verse* edited by Raymond Wilson, reprinted by permission of Hutchinson Books Ltd; *The Snowflake* by Walter de la Mare, reprinted by permission of The Literary Trustees of Walter de la Mare and The Society of Authors as their representative; *"One I love, two I love . . ."* (Anon) from *The Young Puffin Book of Verse,* reprinted by permission of Penguin Books Ltd; the first verse of *Spring Poem* by Raymond Wilson from *Rhyme and Rhythm (Blue Book)* edited by Gibson and Wilson, reprinted by permission of Macmillan, London and Basingstoke; *"The first of May is garland day . . ."* from *A Calendar of Country Customs* by Ralph Whitlock, reprinted by permission of B T Batsford Ltd; *"The rabbit has a charming face . . ."* from *The Private Life of the Rabbit* by R M Lockley, reprinted by permission of Andre Deutsch Ltd; *Time Child* by Gareth Owen from *Salford Road* (Kestrel Books) page 79, copyright © 1971, 1974, 1976, 1979 by Gareth Owen, reprinted by permission of Penguin Books Ltd; *The Frog* by Hilaire Belloc, reprinted by permission of Duckworth and Company; the first verse of *The Kingfisher* by W H Davies, from *The Complete Poems of W H Davies*, reprinted by permission of the Executors of the W H Davies Estate and Jonathan Cape Ltd; second verse of *Fine Weather for Ducks* by Raymond O'Malley from *The Tree in the Wood (Book 3),* reprinted by permission of Granada Publishing Ltd; *To a Squirrel at Kyle-na-no* by W B Yeats, reprinted by permission of Michael Yeats and Macmillan London Ltd; the first verse of *Beech Leaves* by James Reeves from *The Wandering Moon* copyright © James Reeves 1950, reprinted by permission of William Heinemann Ltd; *Winter Morning* by Ogden Nash, reprinted by permission of Curtis Brown London on behalf of the estate of Ogden Nash; four lines from *Snow Poem* by Walter de la Mare, reprinted by permission of The Literary Trustees of Walter de la Mare and the Society of Authors as their representative.

The publishers have made every effort to trace the copyright holders. If we have inadvertently omitted to acknowledge anyone we should be most grateful if this could be brought to our attention for correction at the first opportunity.